CONTENTS

LIBRARIES NI
WITHDRAWN FROM STOCK

INTRODUCTION

The success of our previous books, 'Talking Proper', 'The 'Dictionary of Ulster Posh Speak', and 'The Revised Dictionary of Ulster Posh Speak', confirms our conviction that even in this yobbish age there is a hunger for a touch of culture and good breeding.

The fact that our other books have sold out completely has inspired this new expanded edition combining the best of the 'prectice' sections of all our books and an expanded vocabulary. We aim, through this dictionary, to get to those areas of pretension other dictionaries cannot reach.

The desire for gentility first appeared in the northern portion of Ireland, known as the Province of Ulster and has spread far beyond its confines. In the past one knew that people who did not live in Belfast's Cherryvelly or on The Malone Road were beyond the Pale, socially speaking. They could be guaranteed to speak with a common touch. However, Posh-speak has been carried far beyond this Province and may be found in enclaves such as Derry's Culmore, Dublin's Dort region, from Chicago to Edinburgh and from Southampton to Christchurch, with only slight variations to allow for climatic changes that can affect the nasal passages. We are proud of the contribution our homeland has made to world culture. The world's upper crust, are united by Posh-Speak. No matter where you live this is a guide to polite living, a true guide to what is now a universal language. Ulster Posh-speak is perhaps the most noteworthy contribution made by the people of Northern Ireland to world culture. Study of these pages will enable you to acquire the manner of speech acceptable among the kind of people who attend the Grand Opera House even when there's an opera on, to be unquestionably 'top draw'. We have written phonetically to enable readers to practise as they read. We strongly recommend reading this work aloud.

The value of our work is perhaps best expressed by a lady who wrote to thank us for opening up a whole new world for her. She had 'Never seen a Belly before' and was inspired by our words to go and see 'Swan Lake' performed live. 'Ay was epsolutely enraptured,' writes E.K. of Belfast. 'Aye cried may ays out. It was so sed when thet duck died. Ay couldn't look at orange sauce for a month efterwords.'

No one could ask for a more touching testimonial.

VOCEBULORY

*In speech with a touch of Kless there are no
'common' words.
Not if you say them right.*

The main problem of compiling a posh speak dictionary is that the **'A'** section is almost non-exsistent. The **'A'** sound is not acceptable and tends to be replaced by an **'E'** or an **'O'**.

For instance **'Abbey'** is pronounced **'Ebby'** and **'Ardvark'** is **'Ordvork'**. Even words that sound the same can have totally different meanings. *For example - To most of us 'toll' is what a bell does. But in posh speak it means over six foot.* Sten is not a gun, but short for Stenley, as in Sten Laurel and Oliver Hardy.

We have compiled a list of words, phonetically spelt, with a guide to their meaning as an aid to learning.

Ai	Name for oneself
Acelend	very cold plece, in the sea near whur the Titenic senk
Bailonce	whot mai Hairy loses when he has a drop too much to drink
bay-bay	farewell
beck	the opposite of front

beck of beyond	Cullybeckey, Cestlebarr
bedreggled	whot happens til mai hair when Ai've been cought in the rain
beheve	whot young people kent do today
bellet	type of dence, usually seen in Operor Houses, one laikes to be seen wotching
bellyhoo	ai lot if nonsense
belmy	sort of etmosphere common in Mediterainean climates
bemboo	fesheneble plent one hes in the gorden thet penders eat
bendit	Jessie James
bendit-one orm	thet chep Dr Kimble was efter in 'The Fugitive'.
benk	building thet houses thieves thet steal one's money while pretending to look efter it
benker	person one would be heppy to invite to a porty, in one's home, but would count the spoons efterward
benns	whot wos read out in mai day in church when one wonted to merry. Nowadays the rescles don't bother merrying. They jest live in sin. Desgusting, Ai call it.

8

bleck   the opposite of white

breg   boast

brek   whot mai friend Veroniker did til hur leg when she fencied yon man in Itoly, rushed down the steps efter him, tripped end fell.

bremble   nesty prickly bush which hes bleck fruits that pore people eat in autumn

bren   whot youngsters leck nowdeys

bep   small loaf

bor   place whur one drinks elcohol

ceb   whot stors in movies call a texi

cebby   ai texi driver

cebbege   common vegetable

ceckle   type of leff

chempain   type of elcoholic drink one hes et a porty or celebretion

cherecter   excuse mede for bed beheviour, es in 'he wos ai cherecter'
(*He wos a bed rescol if you esk me.*)

coronory   hort etteck

corporol low type of ormy chep. Not worth bothering with

Cosseck the type of Russien who dences on his hunkers

Deffodils cheerful yellow flowers Wordsworth laiked

dehlyers gorden flowers. Choose the type with posh names such as 'The Bishop of Lenduff'.

demege whot mai Hairy says Ai do til his budget

disester what happens if mai Hairy sees mai benk bellence

edvisor someone who thinks they know whot you should do, but they heven't a notion. (*See also Fenecial Edvisor.*)

edvertise whot hussies, laike mai friend Veroniker do when they wont to get a man. Split skirts so they cen flesh thur knickers, low necklines end hur dyed blonde.

efter the opposite of before

efternoon the port of the day between lunch end dinner when one cen heve tea

elcohol drink which should be taken with cur.

elcoholic	person who makes a hebit of drinking too much elcohol
ellergy	skin resh one gets from eating too many resberries
ellemoney	well deserved regular peyment pore women get of husbands who were bed rescels
enemia	good excuse for not doin anything es one is too tired
enemel	hairy creatures laike kets end poler burrs
enemenor	unmentioneble thing they do to you in hospitals if you dur sey 'No' til a nurse when she esks you 'Did you go?' Go whur? Ai esk you? If you went you maight meet unsuiteble people.
enesthetic	knock out drops
epperition	a ghost
eribs	the cheps who shot Gery Cooper in 'Beau Jest'
essignation	furtive meeting
febricete	meke up a nesty piece of gossip end spread it eround
febulous	see fentestic
feble	wee story

fece front port of head, whot one does ones best to improve. Thet's colled 'putting a good fece on the world'

fect something thet is ebsolutely true, es in, 'it's a proven fect'

feke whot pore gurls wear when they kent efford real jewels

feshill whot every gurl needs regularly to keep hur in good nick

femily ones relatives, some of whom one could well do without

fenencial edvisor a shork who takes one's money end bites lumps out of it

fentestic see febulous

form where a former lives

former chep who grows kerrots end kettle end things out in the country

Glediolers toll spikes of flowers that teke a long time to grow

glemour whot Berberer Stenwick end Susen Heyword hed, but these new young ectresses will never hev, no metter how much they flesh thur knickers

gerrot — sort of ettic, whur pore but interesting people, such es poets, ortists end musicians, live

ges — comporetively cheap fuel used to light stoves end heat houses end oportments

glence — a wee look

glesses — whot one wears when one wonts til see something

greduate — fools who west time going til university, running up debts, costing thur pore perents ai fortune while they drink end pley eround. They should be out urning a living although university is socially eccepteble

gress — green plent used to make lawns in the gorden

gorment — whot any woman needs plenty of to wur til keep hur end up

gorden — plents in the lorge spece around your house

gordener — person who gets paid too much for destroying the plents in your gorden

gornish — porsely, bits of green stuff thet look laike seaweed end so on

chefs	in posh resteronts use to decorete your plete hoping they won't notice they hev not put much on it
gorter	whot bed women end brides wur on the top of thur stockings
grend	word used till describe something thet is ebsolutely magnificent es in 'Grend Opera', Grend Hotel, or grendchild
grendstend	not a very grend place whur one goes til watch a rugby metch if you hev a relative playing
gretitude	whot one hordly ever gets from one's children
gress	green plents whot grow in gordens end golf courses
hebit	something one does often
heggle	whot one hes to do with foreigners when one buys things in markets where you hev til shout very loud before they ken understend English
heggord	looking turrible
hellibut	a fish
helo	shiny thing whot engles hev eround thur heds

heke	a fish
hemmer	a tool for tepping nails in with
hemsters	wee rets thet some people keep as pets, but not in our Pork, thenk God
hend	the port of your orm with fingers on it
heng	whot they should do with thim rescels thet brek intil peoples houses end steal works of ort they kin't appreciate enyway
herress	ennoy
hork	old fashioned word for til listen, as in 'Hork the Herold Angels Sing' or 'Hork, Hork the Lork
illogicol	whot men are. Thurs no sense in them
imege	how one looks
imeginetion	whot men hev too much of when they see a big blonde gurl
immigrete	go end live in a foreign country like the pore storving Irish hed til do during The Grete Femine
immorel	wot the young pople are todey, living with each other end them not merried. Mai mother would hev hed ai fut.

15

Jeg	prick
jengle	ennoyed, es in mai nurves whur jengled
Jenuory	first month in the year
jezz	type of music played by bleck people. Louee Ormstrong played end seng jezz
jow	port of fece whot drops when one hears ai bit of juicy skendol
jugulor	big vein in the neck. If it's cut the person bleeds til death
Kengeroo	a big enimal thet hops
keepseke	something precious thet a man gives you, laike ai ring, thet one does not give beck if one folls out with him
kessel	whur the Royel Femily live when they're not et the Pelis
kindergorden	pley school for children whose perents ken efford it
kitching	whur the cooker end sink are kept
korki	colour of ormy uniforms
kormor	fete. Personelly Ai do not believe in it.
kresh	eccident

16

lebel	wee piece of peper, plestic, or metol for writing names on
lebiol	rude port of the femele body one is better forgetting ebout
lebour	whot pore women hev til go through til hev bebies
leckey	someone to do oll the jobs you don't feel laike doing
lecquer	whot one puts on one's hur
leff	expression of amusement, as in, 'We leffed til thur wosn't ai dray seat in the house.'
ledle	ai type of lorge spoon for serving liquids
ledy	female who knows how til beheve
leger	beer drunk bai louts
lems	little beby sheep, delicious with mint sauce
lepse	whot one's memory does when one forgets how much money one hes spent
levender	plent which ken be turned into the type of perfume thet Ai would not buy. It does not heve a designer label
levish	very expensive entertaining when someone important colls end you hire caterers

17

lipperd — ai big spotted ket thet lives in the jungle whose fur used til meke a posh coat, then thim green people objected

lorceny — whot one's benk meneger does when he tekes money out of one's eccount

lorch — type of tree

lorder — wee room off the kitching in old houses

lorge — Shieler Meckenzie, she's like the Michelin Man

lorgo — boring piece of music written bai Hendle thet one is likely to hear when one is seen et a concert

lorvo — nesty wiggly wee beby thing thet cen turn into a frog, or a butterfly or a fly or some nesty creepy crowly

Mecedem — whot roads are mede from

meceroon — type of wee cake

mecoroni — type of foreign food Italians eat, God help them

medem — Lady of the House

merethon — a long boring race

merrygolds — common ennuel flower with flowers like dendelions

Morch	the month thet comes efter Februory
mep	peper, which mey be so lorge thet it is folded. It tells you whur pleces are
ort	decent pictures of people with clothes on in galleries, end not thet Picesso rubbish where the models look they've been in a terrible eccident
Pender	big bleck end whiote enemel thet eats bamboo shoots end lives in Chiner where thur's not much else til eat
penic	how Ai feel when mai Hairy sees mai benk stetement
pettio	plece til sit in the gorden, usually peved
porking	whot happens in a cor when it is not moving
porty	see levish
rebbi	a Jewish vicar
rebbit	a cute wee enimel thet makes a very good stew
regtime	old time music
rep	modern dence music with no tune end words you kent make out

Scendel	something ebosuletly shameful you know ebout somebody thet is grend fun til chet ebout et a Bridge porty (*See also slender.*)
seck	a big beg
semon	delicious pink fish
senk	whot the Titanic did
shork	thet big fish thet ate all the ectors in 'Jaws'. (*See also Fenecial Edvisor.*)
slent	a slope
steg	a big Scottish enemel with entlers
stemps	whot one sticks on one's Besildon Bond envelopes
stor	little planets thet light up the sky on clear nights
Tebesco	sauce
tengerine	a wee orange
ten	sunburn
texi	whot one travels in when the cor is in for a service
tin	the number between 9 and 11

romence   Mills en Boon, whot pore gurls believe
                   until the get married

tremitised   very very upset

verbener   gorden plent with long stems end wee
                   purple flowers on top

wayne   elcoholic beverege

Some common people

VERY USEFUL WORDS

These words cen be used to mean different things...so...if you want to tolk with a bit of cless you will find them very useful. They are worth mestering.

Of course, anyone who lives in Bellybeen, or Bellymun, or other low cless places will not hev a clue. It takes intelligence to tolk proper.

Ai often seys thet if only thim politicons had the intelligence to concentrate on how to say things thur would be no more orguing ebout unimportant things, such as wars end the price of housing for pore people.

Bebble	whot a brook does
	whot my friend Veroniker does efter a few gins end limes
beboon	big hairy enemal
	mai benk meneger
beck	the opposite of front
	port of one's enetomy
	returned as 'in beck from the Big Epple
bedger	what one does to people if one wonts something
	ai type of enemal found in 'Wind in the Willows'

bed

the opposite of good

what one sleeps in at night

three-in-a bed is whur dorts players stick thur darts

beg

ketch, such as beg a rich husbond

receptecle designed to hold one's money, makeup end odds end ends

whot one hes under one's eyes if one is up too late

belly

Swan Lake

Prefix for places laike Bellykessel, Bellyheckemore, Bellymena end Belly-Jemes-Duff

the kind of shoes pore people ken't efford

whot one must never scretch in public

one should never even mention it!

bet

a ret with wings that only comes out efter dork

a kind of stick used by men dressed in white to hit their balls

whot people do on horses

bend

a group of cheps one hires to pley music

at a porty who shouldn't be allowed near the elechol beforehand

whot one does when one tries to touch one's toes

bend

a curve in the road whot one cen't see round

beth

name of one of thim pore gurls in 'Little Women'

whot one washes oneself in if one ken't efford a jerkuzzi

bleckout

see dork

whot one has when one's husbend esks whot one has done with his money

besh

whot one gets in one's Volvo if one drives into the garage too fest end hits the freezer kebinet

a type of porty as in 'We're heving a besh' in our house.

,

encouragement to try horder, as in 'Hev a besh et it.'

boll

posh porty where one wears an expensive long dress

round object one cen pley with

bork

whot one's pedigree dog does when fleg sellers rettle your door knocker

the outside port of a tree

get the wrong idea, as in bork up the wrong tree

brece

whot one hes til do before going til see one's benk meneger, es in 'Brece yourself'

whot some pore edelescents hev to wear to make their teeth straight

cebinet

a cupboard

men end women who help the prime minister, or president, ruin the country

celery

whot one's husbend urns

a commom vegetoble, eccepteble but common

clesp

catch the hold of, as in he clesped her in his orms

buckle as in 'the clesp on mai good ballet shoes'

corrol

reef made in worm woters by a wee enemel

singing es in 'Corrol Society'

dork

whot happens when the sun goes down

not know about something as 'I'm in the dork ebout the skendel

when them rescels et the Electricity Board cause a bleckout

dreyvin	whot men do with a big stick when they tee-off when pleying golf
	the type of rain thet comes down by the bucket load and wrecks one's hairdo
	whot one does in a car, one goes dreyving around the countryside
dreft	nesty wind. One does not know where it is coming from, one only knows where it is going
	a benk dreft, a way of sending money for which those robbers in the benk chorge a fortune. Why should they chorge a fortune for you to send your own money somewhere?
ecrobet	circus performers or disco dencers who prance around like med people who read the 'Kemma Sutra'
end	also
	finis (whot foreigners put et the finish of thur boring films)
eround	pley eround as in pley eround of golf
	heve ai fency man (or woman) as in pley eround, heve a lover
	spread eround as in gossip

ent

the wife of one's uncle

nesty wee creepy crawley one might be unfortunate enough to meet   in a gorden

eskeloppes

type of edible sea food

very thin slice of meat

euphorier

feshioneble gorden plent with peculier green flowers

very heppy, over the moon

ex

husbend one hes finished with, who peys elemony (*A husband one hes finished with who does not pey elemony is not worth mentioning.*)

whot lumberjacks use to cut trees down

fen

a loyal edmirer

electric thing that birls round end cools you

fency

surprise as in 'fency thet? or 'she hes a 'fency man' something one would like, as in 'a little of what you fency does you good

flesh

vulgor

a quick look

whot one grows a bit much of as one grows older

geng   bed people who mug innocent strengers

A lorge gang, like the Mefia sell drugs

a group of silly old men, laike mai Hairy who go away for week-ends to play golf

heff   fifty percent, or fifty five percent, explained as heff end a wee bit, which is the very least a decent woman should eccept from her husbend's celery

ennoyed, as she went ewey in a heff

hem   a type of becon

the way febric is sewed to keep it from freying

hendicep   something to do with golf, a socially eccepteble game. (*Ai do not pley myself. Ai do not like getting may hur wrecked walking in the rain.*)

something wrong with somebody, laike a smoll selery

Jecket   short designer coat
throw in the towel as in 'jecket it in.'

jem   whot one mekes from the resberries from one's gorden

what heppens when towns end cities become so full of cors end lorries thet one sits in the treffic end kent go shopping, one's in a treffic jem

lep

jump, as in lept up

lick as in 'kets like to lep milk'

a type of dence bed women do

lesh

long stiff hairs on eyelids, used til flutter et men

whot bed men end women do to each other with a whip

whot a crocodile could do with its tail - lesh out with it end knock you down

lest

model of a foot use to make very posh shoes

keep going until the job is done, such as shopping

be et the end of a queue

letch

wee metal thing thet keeps a door, or gate, shut

heng on, like Chorlie Ebernethy did to me et the porty last Fridey night. Ai couldn't get rid of him end he wos only efter the one thing

lether

foam

sweat end feel uncomfortable, as in 'she wos oll in a lether'

letitude

the lines thet go eround the world

rope as in 'give her enough letitude end she'll heng hurself'

ley	people who go to church who are not members of the clergy
	chase a ghost
	put down
	what hens do
merry	heppy as in 'Heppy Christmas'
	hed too much to drink, 'she wos a trifle merry.'
Pem	gurl's name
	the Sundey before Easter
	tree that cen grow in sheltered, frost free gardens end tropical places
pen	whot one fries hem end eggs in
	whot one ken write with
perish	die
	whot the vicor is in charge of
pet	cute wee enemel one loves, like a pedigree ket or a poodle dog
	what one has on toast as a starter to a meal
Pevlova	the greatest belly dencer who ever lived
	a type of delicious pudding invented by the ebove belly dencer
	dogs trained by the ebove belly dencer in her spur time

seck

ai big beg
being told one's services are no longer
required

seedy

suspicious looking person who looks pest
thur sell-by date

one on thim wee, shiny records thet won't
sit on a proper gremophone

send

whot beaches are made of

tell someone til go aiwey

post a letter or a porcel

slender

Kate Moss

things you say ebout your friends behind
their backs at Bridge porties

does not have a lot of money as in 'of
slender means'.

pork

an excepteble, but common, type of meat

where one lives, port of one's eddress

where one goes for a wolk

what one has to do with the car when
one goes shopping

wotch

posh jewellery that tells the time,
designed by Guggi, or someone of that ilk

look out as in 'wotch yourself'
keep looking to see if you can see
somebody, or something

USEFUL PHRASES FOR CHET

*Egnes Hairiot Johnston has kindly suggested
the following phrases for use by those
who would laike til add
<u>a bit of cless</u> to conversations.*

Phrase	Translation
You heff ti lleff	So what!
Ectuelly thet's not raight	I disagree with you
Thet's ebsolutely febulous	I am jealous. Watch out!
Et's fundamentol	Anything to do with money
Ay laike the ombeonce	It's expensive
You don't sey?	So what!
Thet's turrible!	I'm enjoying what you are saying
He hes a good celery	He is worthy of respect, he is/was a 'good catch' that is a good marriageable prospect
Et's a loverleee little house	I am jealous of your home
Ectuelly, she looks laike an ebsolute tort	She's better looking than either of us

You're ebsolutely sweeeet!   I can't stand you
Ai only hurd thet letely end   This is the latest piece
may hur hes been curled!   of juicy scandal

No both room is complete
without a jerkuzi   Top that if you can!

Hev a wee sherry end a bit
of semon petty   I am the perfect hostess

Thon woman's got a face
laike a corduroy jecket   She has a few wrinkles

Aim ebsolutely traumatised   I've had a slight shock

He wus rentin end raven   He was scolding

PRECTESS WITH EGNES

Now we move from the theory to the practical -
or 'prectical as you will learn to say.

Reading proper talk in not enough. You have to practise speaking it aloud in front of a mirror.

Why the mirror? Because it is essential to watch the shape of your mouth as you speak. The golden rule to remember is that it is bad manners to speak with your mouth open. As we explained in our previous educational thesis *Talking Proper*, you must pucker your lips as if you are about to whistle then talk *'through the wee gap in the middle'*.

The only drawback to this is that when you approach someone who is unfamiliar with posh speak, with your lips already puckered for action, they may become startled, thinking you are about to kiss them.

The mirror is also useful to practise the birdlike head movements and facial expressions that give posh speak its unique advantage in communication over thet tawdry Information Super Highway. Indeed it is doubtful if the Internet could distribute a juicy bit of gossip faster than that doyen of Cherryvelly society, Mrs. Egnes Johnston.

Once you have the mirror in place, practise these typical conversations.

PRECTESS ONE

Remember Everil Connor, the plump wee girl thet merried Cuthbert Conner of the Benn Velly Connors, the one with the bed eyesight end fet enkles? Fet as a butcher's ket, she was. Well she reng till say thet she's moving intil a new bingalow in a feshionable port of Bellyheckemore. I hed till tell her "God bless your cotton socks, Everil, there is **NO** feshionable port of Bellyheckemore "

PRECTESS TWO

While we were in Frence lest weekend. Hairy insisted we went up till the top of the Effel Tor. Ay didn't want till go because it was eposlutely leshing down. We don't get rain like thet in Cherryvelley you know. It was pelting down so herd it gethered in the guttering of may new Peris hot end spleshed all over may Belly shoes, the ten ones with the gold clesp. They were eposlutely soaked. You would hev thought I'd stepped in a poodle.

PRECTESS THREE

If you ever get invited to visit Emenda McKendless at her flet on the Melone Road, which is hordly likely, but you niver know, for God's sake don't let her give you any of her dendylion wayne. It's ebsolutely guestly. It's like embemming fluid. But it's all you'll be offered, so wotch yourself. Emenda went till a big tent one night end got Born Again, she says. Won't let real elcohol pess her lips. End when you remember whit she was like when we were all schoolgirls at Eshleigh. Used to drink the cooking sherry et domestic science cless end fill the bottle up with ink and tep woter.

Remember the gym teacher hed to be rushed till hospital when her mouth went all bleck end they thought she'd caught something tropical on the school trip to Bellyhelbert. Thet deft school nurse was going till give us all injections against Bleckwoter fever, before Emenda broke down end confessed.

She would hev been expelled for thet except the teaching steff would hev hed till explain what they were doing with the bottle in the Steff Room.

Enyway, you wouldn't recognise Emenda now. Gone all Holy she has. Doesn't like sin at all anymore. End she used till be so fond of it. Do you remember her beck in the old days when we'd all put on our gled-regs end head for the Boat Club on a Setterday night?

The Boat Club was on an island then. They tied a wee punt on a rope you were pulled across on.

Emenda just loved those dences. End she always wore white

underwear so it would show through when them blue lights came on for the dencing. She was a bit of a tort in her day. Thet's where she met her first husband. Erchie whatisname? A toll, hendsome chep who played the clerinet in the bend. Remember they nearly drowned. They were snogging thet hord on the punt thet it overturned end lended on top of them. They hed till dreg the river for his cor keys end they niver did find her underwear.

We leffed end leffed thet night. Ah. Heppy Days!

DENCING IN THE DORK

by Billy Simpson

"Hello. Is thet you Sendra? Its your sister Egnes from Cherryvelly. You sound breathless. What hev you been doing? Niver mind. I'm ringing to see if your electricity is off?

"Its a total bleckout here, end we were wondering if your Semi could bring us over a wee flesk of hot woter for a cup of tea. Oh! Ballybeen is blecked out too.

"I know. Its epsolutely skendelous. If I'd known a wee storm could bleck out the country I'd never hev got Hairy to buy thim NIE shures.

"What? Oh! You and Semi went till bed to keep worm. Thets why you're out of breath? Oh! OH! Sendra really!

"No Hairy and I hev not gone till bed. We're sitting here surrounded by more kendles then the Veticen. We've been hevin' a wee gless of ShetoNuveDePep. Thet's wayne you know. From a bottle. Not thet stuff you buy in a box with a wee tep.

"Ectually its been quate romentic. We put on the radio end they were playing Net King Cole records, so Hairy and me were hevin' a wee dence. Hee Hee Hee. Yeaasss.

"Dencing in the dork,

"Till the tune ends,

"Wur dencing in the dork"

"Ay think the wayne was going till Hairy's head. He got quate effectionate. It took me beck till the Queen's Hop in the 1950s. Thet's whur I met Hairy. He was stending by the bendstend end he looked just like Deekie Velentine except for the bold petch and the big ears.

"Oh you're right, it was Denis Lotus. Deekie was the fet one. Enyway we didn't dence for very long. There was this wild epperition appeared at the French windows, teppin to be let in. It was thet Veronicer from next door. You know, the widow with the blonde rinse. Well, she came in and plenked herself down between me and Hairy on the sofa and said she was too fraytoned to stay on her own in the dork.

"Thet one fraytoned?!! Her thet broke thet man's leg at the Jenuary sales. Thet'll be the day. "Enyway she was all over may Hairy and he's so easy till get round when he's hed a few. He was leffing and telling her how young she looks.

'Oh' she siz, 'You are lucky thim lights are out or you'd see may lefter lines.'

"LEFTER LINES? The woman's got a face like a corduroy jecket. So I sez, sweet as you like, well if them's lefter lines, it must hev been a helluva joke. You must hev been trepped in a lift with Frenk Corson.'

"Well she give this dray leff end a glure you could skate on. Drenk heff a bottle of may gin end went home in a huff. Thet Veronicer was always a bitch. She was chasing other men before poor Edgar was cold in his urn. She was always like thet. Remember we used to see her swenking around at the dences in Romenos yerrs ago. She was the same then. Ay remember well thet night she came till me afraid she'd got pregnant. She said 'Egnes, Ay don't know how it heppened. It must hiv been something in the air thet night.' Yeasss, Ay thought. Your legs by the sound of it.

"Enyway Sendra, I'll let you get beck till your bed. Hairy's laying beck here on the sofa soun' till the world. When he wakes with all these kendles round him, he'll think he's died if I'm not thur till let him see he's not in heaven yet".

THE LEND WE BELONG TILL IS GREND

By Billy Simpson

"Sendra. Is thet you? Oh thenk God you're home. Veronicer and Ay are epsolutely traumatised. You'll never believe whit heppened at the Cherryvelly Dremetic Society tonight.

"Whit heppened? You might well esk? Veronicer is here with me. She daren't go home in the state she's in. She's on teblets that don't mix with gin. At least not with a quart of it.

"But whit a night we hev hed. We were et rehearsals for the Dremetic Society's Christmas Concert. We're not doing a pento this yerr. Instead its going to be a tribute to the music of Roger Hemmerstein.

"Who? Rogers and Hemmerstein. Oh. They're two cheps are they? Well, its whoever wrote 'South Pacific'. Enyway, Veronicer and Ay were stending in the chorus heppily singing away at Oklahomo...

"We know we belong till the lend.
End the lend we belong till is grend."

"Suddenly this new young director they've hired fer the show jumps up and screams 'STOP! STOP! STOP THE MUSIC.'

"Veronicer and Ay were mystified because it sounded grend till us. Next thing he pointed right et us and esk the two of us till come to the front of the stage.

"Yiss," I said. "Whit is it Mr Director?"

"What do you think you are doing?" he said, all sercestic like.

"How do you mean?" I says. (Veronicer didn't say anything because her teblets were storting till fight with the gin she'd hed earlier.)

"That hand jive thing?" he said.

"Oh you mean holding our fingers in the air and swinging our heads from side till side?" Ay said. "We saw thet et a Berry Menelow concert, only they did it with kendles. We thought it would edd till the presentation."

"He shook his head and said thet we were supposed till be rough, tough frontier cowgirls not Berry Menelow groupies.

"You must be robust and YIP and slap your thighs when you sing this song", he says.

"Slep wur thighs?" I said. "But we don't slep wur thighs in Cherryvelly. Thets whit Germans do. We didn't even slep wur thighs when we did The Sound of Music' end thur wur Netzies in thet."

"He gives us a funny look and says, "Really" he says.

"Well why are the pair of you are dressed like gipsy fortune tellers?"

"We are NOT gipsy fortune tellers," Ay told him, "These ur serongs. We dressed like this because we thought we were going till be singing 'Belly High' from 'South Pacific'. We thought it would odd till the tropical etmosphere."

"This is when he threw his head intil his hends and said there was no such song as 'Belly High'.

"Yis there is," I said. "The one the big fet woman sings till the sailors...

"Belly High will call you
Eny night or day
Belly High dah de dah de dah".

"Thet one," I said, thinking pore Roger Hemmerstein must be turning in his grave.

"Well! He slepped this clip board down on the chair and it crecked like a pistol shot. We all jumped beck.

"Its not Belly High," he shouted. "Its BALI HI! BALI HI! BALI...BALI...BALI. Come on say it. BAAA-LI HI. BAAAA-LL"

"Thets not the South Pacific" I said. "Thets more like East Entrim."

"He went all cold, efter I said thet. He glurred et me and said in one of thim voices you could cut a Veda with... "What does the word Belly mean to you?"

"Well netturally Ay said... "SWAN LAKE."

"Well he went epsolutely beserk. Rentin end raven like a THING possessed. Threw his clip board et the pianist and screamed something about working with cretins. Aren't thim the wee furry things in thet Steven Spielberg picture?

"Enyway by this time Ay was beside myself with rage. This young out-of-work theatrical coming till Cherryvelly with his page-boy hurrcut and talking till Veronicer and me like thet in front of everybody. Efter all the years Ay've given till the Orts in Cherryvelly. If it wasn't for may Hairy paying for the costumes they've hev hed till hev done 'Ennie Get Your Gun' in thur shifts.

"And Sendra you know ay hev always been very ortistic. Remember Ay played the lead in The Berrets of Wimpole Street' et Eshliegh.

"Whit? Elizabeth Browning? No No. NOT her. Ay was Mr. Berrett. Remember efterwords the Dremer Critic of the 'Northern Whig' said Charles Laughton wasn't a petch on me when it came till frightening an audience. Ay still hiv thet cutting somewhere. Ah heppy days.

"Enyway, thet wasn't the worst of it. Ay grebbed Veronicer and led her beck till the dressing room and swore thet when Ay saw medim chairman of the Dremetic Society thet young upstort would be sent pecking.

"Ay couldn't wait till get out of thet serong end thet bleck make-up. The more Ay thought of us stending there singing Oklahomo dressed like slave girls, the defter ay felt. It was Veronicer's idea. Ay should niver hiv listened till her. She just wanted till wear thet revealing two-piece thet shows her navel. End Ay should niver hiv let her talk me intil puting on thet bleck make-up. It won't wash off! We've tried everything from shempoo till Flesh Liquid end it won't shift. When Ay took off may serong Ay looked like a Penda but Veronicer looks like a pedestrian crossing".

THE CHERRYVALLY ECEDEMY OF SPEECH AND DRAMER

By Billy Simpson

"Hello Sendra. Ifs me. Yer sister Egnes from Cherry velly. Tell you whit I'm ringing about. Remember thet big het I lent youse for Gledys McCorkills wedding. The big bleck one that Deddy said made you look like Barney Eastwood.

"Whit?? Oh Clint Eastwood was it? Ur they not the same person? Ay thought thet ector in "Dirty Hairy" became a boxing meneger efter he lost his looks.

"Oh they're two different people? Well you live end learn don't you.

"Enyway I need the het beck for Winsday efternoon. Its the only one thet goes with may new shoes. I'm not supposed to tell you this but your big sister hiz been appointed to the Board of Governors of Cherryvelly Ecedemy of Speech end Dramer.

"Yeaass. Its hord to believe efter all these yerrs. Its like a dream come true.

"Apparently it was a toss up between me end Gloria Hunniford but she's not one of the ecedemy's old girls you know. A lot of people think she is -but no. She niver came to our klesses. She's just a nettural.

"Netalie Bredshaw rang me lest night efter the governors emergency meeting. Apparently there wiz a big row end Medge Corter resigned in a huff.

"She sid the ecedemy was wasting its time in Cherryvelly because we already talk proper. She wanted till open the klesses to pore people.

"Lord knows, Sendra, you kin't call me a snob but we kin't

hiv a lot of riff-reff coming in. Cor salesmen, radio personelities end thet.

"I expect they're not bed people but would you sit in a chair efter one of them? Ay think not. No ay think we should keep the Ecedemy as a centre of excellence for budding ectors and ectresses from Cherryvelly. "But Netalie siz you couldn't reason with Medge Corter when she gets a bee in her bonnet. Netalie sid Medge stormed out saying she was off till Bellymena till set up her own speech klesses end do some missionary work.

"Well! Ay'll say this for Medge. She's not afraid of a chellenge. You heff till leff.

"Enyway the first meeting of the new Board is nixt Winsday end all the lady governors wear hets et the meetings. It's a bit like church without the collection.

"Oh thet reminds me Sendra, did youse know thet poor Clure Kemeron died suddenly? Remember, she wiz et Eshleigh with us? Big girl. Played goalkeeper fer the hockey team before she was expelled. You must remember her?

"Her second husband owned thet travel company thet sold time-shurs in Trensylvenia.

"Somebody said it was a skiing eccident. Poor Clure fell off the Metterhorn end they didn't find her for six months. Yeaass. But the snow kept her perfectly fresh for the funeral. Would you be without a freezer efter hearing thet?   "Her husband flew her beck till Belfast lest Setterday.

"I meant to go, but it was jist one of those days whin I wasn't| in the mood for a funeral. Netelie and Medge were at it. They were supposed till sketter her eshes in the shoe department of Enderson end McAuley's but its shut now end when it opens again its going to hiv Mickey Mouse in it.

"Netelie didn't think Clure would hiv wanted till be trempted over by people dressed like big retts, so they jist skettered the eshes outside Yeegers".

45

GORING, SKIBOO AND KENABIS

by Billy Simpson

It's your sister Egnes from Cherryvelley. Ectually ay was ringing to thenk you and Semi for coming down to the police station lest week and getting Veroniker end me out. Ay expect the Chief Inspector gave thet young constable a bit of his mind for herressing innocent women just because we forgot to tell thim our cor wasn't stolen efter all. What... oh well yes. End for heving an out of date driving licence. Yes, yes, yes. Alright! End an expired tex disc. But it was all a misunderstending. Could heppen to anyone. Enyway it only took thet inspector faive minutes to realise we weren't the type of persons to steal a cor. End certainly not a second hend one.

It turns out the inspector knows may Hairy from the Buffelos... Or is it Mooses? They're in the same Teepee or something . Ay kin niver keep trek of all these clubs Hairy is in. He hes more bedges then Goring... Och Sendra, surely you remember Goring? Thet big fet German thet bombed your Ent Emenda's greenhouse in 1941. He was as famous as Skiboo et the time.

Enyway, when Hairy got beck from his jaunt to Emsterdem end I told him about Veroniker end me getting arrested he leffed end leffed. He phoned his pel, the inspector, end invited him over for lunch lest Tuesday. His name's Petrick but everybody calls him Peddy for short. An awfully nice person. A bit like Inspector Morse only taller end not so crebbit.

46

But the eftemoon nearly turned intil a disester. Apparently Peddy is a keen gordener end was fesenated by some of our exotic plents. He kept esking what they were all called. Well of course ay heven't a clue. Ay reley on our young gordener who comes twice a week. The young chop Veroniker recommended efter our old gordener died heff way through laying down the cement slebs for the patio extension. Yessss. It was tregic. But luckily we got somebody else to come end finish it.

Enyway, efter Hairy end Peddy came in from the gordon, Peddy esked me whit ay knew about Ken Abis? End he was using his Inspector's voice. You know, about four keys lower then normal speaking.

Ay thought. Ken Abis? Ken Abis? Wasn't he Lou Costello's portner. Abis end Costello? No. Thet was Bud Abis. So ay hed till say thet ay didn't know enyone of thet name.

He said it wasn't a person, it was a drug. End it is made from some of the plents in our conservatory. Well! Ay nearly fell off may churr. He pointed out three of the pot plents in the Conservatory end said they were illegal substances.

Ay thought, may god! Ay'm a women of illegal substance. Thet's when it all fell intil place. This young gordenor was coming twice a week to tend these plents and prune the leaves. End he always took the leaves away in his pocket. Sendra! Ay was the accomplice till a drug beron end didn't know it. Peddy said not to worry, but he took the gordener's name and told us to destroy the plents.

Well neturelly ay threw them on the fire. Thet was a mistake because faive minutes later Hairy was doing his Frenkie Lane impression. He storted yelling:

"Head em out, Herd em in,
Whip em off, Kick their ass
Head em off. Bring em beck
Raw-Hiiiide".

Ay hed till dreg him away from the smoke in case he gelloped off across the fields end frightened the kettle.

A RETTLE IN THE NIGHT

by Billy Simpson

"Hello. Hello, (tep-tep-tep). One-Two-Three... Whit's thet constable? Its already tested? Ay just speak intil this wee thing, is thet right?

Now?... You want me to speak now? I see. Well may name is Mrs. Egnes Johnston end ay live at 'Wuthering Cherries', Cherryvelley. Ay ken't remember the postcode but thurr's a B in it if thet's any help.

This is may statement about a break-in at may home lest night. Veroniker, may friend, end next door neighbour, end I, were alone in the house et the time. May husband Hairy heving taken himself off with a geng of his cronies till Portrush for a week till wotch Ornold Pemmer playing golf. Typical. May son, Torquin, was away on some kind of commendo course, climbing cliffs end thet sort of thing. Its a menegement training scheme of some kind for a job in a library. His therapist says Torquin suffers from low self steam, whitever thet is, end climbing mountains is just the thing to put some steam beck intil him.

What's thet constable?... The burgelry? Ay am jist coming till thet, if you'd stop interrupting. Ay am just painting a wee word picture till set the scene. May ay continue?... Thenk you.

Enyway, Veroniker, may neighbour, came over efter dinner till keep me company. She'd hired a video for us till wotch. She

49

likes thim 'Basic Ettrection Instinct' kind of pictures but ay would rether wotch 'Murder She Wrote'. Enyway, she hed this video called The Chippendales' end ay thought it was about thim wee squirrels with the buck teeth. But it wasn't.

What's thet?... You want till hear about the burgelry? Hmmmth! Ay am coming till thet. Well, Veroniker and I were just chetting end heving a few glesses of wayne, late on when I noticed she hed fallen asleep and hed slid off the settee ontil the floor. She does thet sometimes when she drinks wayne on top of gin. Enyway, ay was beginning to doze off in the ormchair mayself when I heard this rettle from upstairs. Like somebody smeshing a window. Then ay heard these footsteps end noises like drawers being rensecked. Ay woke Veroniker end told her whit was heppening.

Now we didn't penic. We crawled on our hends end knees intil the kitchen end Veroniker picked up a fraying pen to use as a club.

Ay found an old air pistol in a drawer, but no pellets. Veroniker hoked through her hendbeg end brought out boxes of vitamin pills she takes end we found one she takes for her skin thet fitted perfectly.

I said "What heppens if I shoot him dead?" Veroniker said "You ken't kill anybody with a vitamin loaded pellet gun. The worst thet could heppen to him is it might clear up his spots "

Just with thet the kitchen door burst open end the burgler was stending there facing me, with may jewellery box under his orm. I screamed "Steek 'em up, SCUMBEG." I knew thet's what you say. I seen it on 'Cegney end Leesy'.

He looked as surprised as me. Then he looked me up end down. Ay hed the gun pointed at him, end he just leffed. LEFFED!! The cheek of it. Neturally I shot him.

But ay only hit his ear-ring. It made a helluva tinkle. Then, before he could do anything else, Veroniker came out from behind the door end smeshed him in the face with the fraying pen.

New the rescel wants Veroniker end me chorged with assault and bettery and demeging the Peace Process. Kin he do thet?

HEVEN'T BEEN IN YONKS

by Billy Simpson

Hello Sendra, Is thet you? It's me, yer sister Egnes from Cherryvelley. You'll niver guess who's home from Keneda.   Gledys McKendless!! Yeaass! The nervous wee girl thet used to live three doors up from us. She is over with her former husband.

What? No. No. Not her ex-husband. He's a former. Owns a big form in Elberta. For heven's sake Sendra, surely you know whit a form is? Its where they grown things. Kettle end kerrots end stuff like thet.

......What? Well it may be a faaaarmer in Bellybeen but he's a former in Cherryvelley. Honestly Sendra, you've storted till tolk very common since you went till live there. You should come over here end visit us et 'Wuthering Cherries' more often end keep in touch with your roots.

Enyway, remember Gledys went off end married thet big toll chep she ren over in her cor outside Belmoral Show Grounds. He was over from Keneda till see our egriculture show beck in the '60s. No. No. He wasn't bedly hurt. He hordly limps at all now. Enyway, she visited him in hospital end they storted a big romence end as soon as he got over his leg they got married. He took her beck till Keneda along with a bull he bought et Belmoral. Well, they're over here till celebrate their 30th wedding enniversary. Yeasss.

It's hord till believe it's 30 years. End she's hordly nervous at all now. Doesn't jump out of her skin nearly as often. Life on the prairie has hordened her. Tolks like a real Yenk. A bit like Marjoire Main in thim hillbilly pictures yerrs ago. But you want to

52

hear her about thim Spenish fishermen. The Kenedians are jist rippin' about thim stealing their fish. Ay told her we in Cherryvelley support Keneda till the hilt. End thet's true Sendra. Ay heven't cooked a Spenish Omelette since this fish wor storted.

But thet's by the by. Gledys end I hed a wee trip down memory lane in Belfast. End I can tell you thet woman is shocked et whit his heppened till this City. Enderson end McAuleys, gone. Robinson end Cleaver, gone. No Brends in the orcade anymore. No Ritz cinema. She said it was like Eglenta in 'Gone With the Wind' efter the Yenkies hed morched through. A whole way of life gone in a flesh. Well ay said it was more then a flesh. I mean she's been away thirty yerrs.

Oddly enough it was the Ritz not being there thet hit her most. She was niver out of thet place. Ay think she used till hev a crush on the organist Stenley Wylie. Remember how excited she used to get when his organ came up through the floor.

Enyway she hed this powerful desire till go to the pictures so we took her till thet new place where they hev heff a dozen screens all showing different pictures. Now ay heven't been till the pictures in yonks. Efter Rock Hudson end Doris Day stopped making them my hort wasn't in it.

Enyway Gledys and I went intil see this Four Weddings end a Funeral' she'd heard so much about. It was alright, ay suppose. Still thet chep Hugh Grent isn't a petch on Kerry Grent, but it was nice to see an ector getting on so well despite thet terrible stemmer. Ay thought he was putting thet on but then I saw him making a speech on television end he's jist as bed in real life. God help him.

I think it must be something to do with political correction thet they're letting a lot of hendikept people stor in pictures now. Ay mean Tom Henks doesn't seem the full shilling end thet Arnold Swartshissname end Sylvester Stalone both hev terrible speech impediments. Yet they're superstors!!!!!? A bit of pressure from the Fair Employment Agency there, I fency.

FENLIGHT FENN -
THE VEMP OF MELONE EVENUE

by Billy Simpson

Hello Sendra, is thet you? Its me. Yer sister Egnes from Cherryvelly. Just ringing to tell you thet my Hairy is in hospital. Yeaasss. I've been worried seek. They didn't hev a private word available and he is in a general word with the pore people. It's eposlutely tregic.

Whits thet Sendra? How is who? Oh Hairy! Oh he'll be alright. He'll be out tomorrow. He'd hev got out today if he hedn't been so dremetic about it. You know whit men orr like when they get a wee bit of pain. All it needs is a bit of a rub and it'll be like a new leg.

Enyway its all his own fault. Even the doctor said he should hev hed more sense. ... Whits thet? Well if you'll heng on a minute Sendra, I'll tell you whit the old ejit was doing. Raising money for cherity, thet's whit. Yeaass. Him end some other old fools from his rugby days were heving a few drinks efter the Rotary lunch when one of thim hed the bright idea of having the Kless of '57 old boys rugby metch to raise money for cherity. Saving Speniards from donkeys or something like thet, I think.

Yeaasss!! A rugby metch! End there wasn't one of thim had been on a rugby field for thirty years. It has been fifteen years

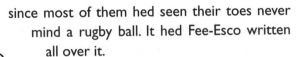

since most of them hed seen their toes never mind a rugby ball. It hed Fee-Esco written all over it.

If you'd seen thim running ontil the pitch. By the time they got to the middle, heff of thim were on their knees gespin' for breath. You'd leff if it wasn't so pethetic.

They hed till get an embulance end a respiratorr for Stenley Edams. You know, Fenny's husband. Whit? .... Oh Sendra! Surely you remember Fenny. From Eshleigh. She was the vemp of Melone Evenue. They used till call her Fenlight Fenny efter thet eccident with the box of metches. Remember she walked funny for a week. Enyway the excitment was too much for Stenley's pacemaker. He never even touched the ball. He just ren efter it for a forty yords end collepsed.

At least Hairy got his injury during the metch. Somebody pessed him the ball and he storted till run up the field. But efter thirty yords the best he could do was walk. Thet was alright because the ones trying till ketch him were walking too by thet stage. They wouldn't hev caught him if he hedn't stopped with a stich in his side. Thet's when they fell on him like a peck of wolves. Not thet they wanted the ball. They jist wanted an excuse till lie down. A whole pile of thim lended on top of him. Hairy said it wasn't the weight that got till him. It was thet he couldn't breathe for the smell of Algipan.

Efterwords he could hordly stend because he'd twisted his knee when he turned round to give somebody beck their dentures thet hed fallen out in the frecass.

Ay told them before they storted thet it would end in tears. The Cordiac Games, we called it. Veroniker and I were watching from the corr. Well it was too cold till stend outside. Enyway the metch was abandoned efter 20 minutes. When the embulance arrived for pore Stenley helf the players wanted till get intil it with him.

Veroniker and I called on Fenny later to see how Stenley was. She said he's awake and talking again. I suppose they just plugged him into the mains while they fixed his betteries. Enyway the first thing he esked Fenny was to remember to tape the "Medness of George the Third" for him on Chennel Four. Fenny said thet was a bit pointless since they hedn't seen the first two episodes. Yeaass. I leffed too. Well, Fenny was niver thet good at history. I told her it wasn't episode three of a serial, it was a film about King George. Fenny said "I niver knew he was med. I thought he just hed a wee bit of a stemmer."

Not our King George, I told her. Not the Queen Mother's husband. It was a film about the olden days. Like "Pride and Prejudice", I said. Fenny says whenever she watches films where people write with feathers, she falls asleep after ten minutes. She blames the minuet music.

56

WE COULDN'T SAVE HENRI'S GOATEE

by Billy Simpson

Hello Sendra, Is thet you? Its yer sister Egnes from Cherryvelly. Just ringing to apologise for you being turned away from may borborcue porty yesterday evening. I want to assure you it wasn't because of you wearing thet tetty old keftan from your hippie years at Woodvale...............What's thet Sendra?.......... It was Woodstock. Well whitever Wood it was, thet era hes pessed. Let it go.

But thet was not why you were turned away. The fire brigade didn't let anyone pest the cordon until they were sure everything was demped down. As you may hev deduced from the presence of two fire engines and a police patrol corr, the entire porty turned intil an epsolute FEE-ESCO. Ay blame Hairy. He wanted a traditional old feshioned borbercue. With hemburgers and fet sausages and things like thet.

Ay told him, "Hairy. Cherryvelly people do not sit around in a gorden eating burnt mince in a bep. We are not seveges." Ay mean, God knows what wayne you'd serve with hemburgers. No, ay insisted on heving a catered affair with vol-u-vonts, semon petty and wee dips for your cheesy biscuits. And ay wanted it catered by Henri of Bellymacarrett. Y'know Henri was on TV lest

57

month. Yeaas. On one of thim morning shows whurr they cook one minute and tolk about PMT the next.

Hairy said a catered borborcue missed the point of the thing but ay spoke to Henri's live-in-portner on the phone and he said Henri could do both and rettled off a lovely menu list with everything from marinaded wild duck to tuna steaks. Plus all the wee dips as well. Neturally I told him to forget the tuna. Ay mean. Come on. Thet's whit Veroniker next door feeds till her ket.

Well, Sendra, everything was going tickitty-boo until they tried to light the chorcoal. It must hev been kept in a demp corner all winter because it just wouldn't ketch fire. Henri said he hed something in his ven thet would stort it. But while he was away Hairy poured some lighter fluid over it. Then Veroniker hed the bright idea of pouring some of may good Napoleon Brendy over it. And when Henri came beck he sprayed it with something else.

WELL! When Henri stuck a match to it the whole thing went WOOF. The flames leaped ten feet in the air; took off poor Henri's eyebrows and thet wee goatee beard he used to hev. He'd hev lost his pigtail too if Hairy hedn't beat it out with a spetula. The fire brigade were called when the flames from the hedge set fire to the Herrison's cherry tree. They live the other side of us from Veroniker. Nice people but netrually a bit upset. But as I pointed out, thet tree was for two toll enyway. And they hev a for better view of East Belfast now.

.................Whit's thet Sendra?............... Oh whit heppened to Henri? Well, Hairy and I drove him to the RVH kesualty deportment to see if his goatee could be saved. Sedly it couldn't. But thet's the first time ay hev see thet big new tin building they are putting up to replace the old hospital. It's not open yet but it should be nice when it's finished. The front looks a bit like the keptain's bridge on one of thim big oil tenkers thet are always running aground and poluting the seagulls.

GORDON PARTY AT THE KESSEL

by Billy Simpson

"It's me. Yer sister Egnes from Cherryvelly. Jist ringing till tell you about may day out et the Royal Gordon Porty et Hillsboro kessel.

"Yeaass. Moi end Hairy got invited but it wiz a secret. We couldn't even tell you and Semi. It was an epsolutely perfect efternoon, except for the rain, the mud and me het blowing away. We hid till park miles away fer security reasons and they took us to the kessel in a bus.

"End you know me end buses? I couldn't get on a Citybus without two vellium end a wee gin. But this was different. None of the riff-reff thet looks like they're used till buses.

"In fect everybody looked like they'd niver seen a bus in thur lives before. We were all stending thurr in our big flowered hets waiting for the driver till lower a remp or something but he told us we hed till get on without it.

"When we got till the kessel this big security gord tried till search me. I told him there wus no need because me end Hairy were from Cherry velly, but he sid it didn't metter if we were from the Sen Fernendo Velly, we hed till be searched.

"Well, who wus the first one I bumped intill? VERONICER!

"Yeasss! Her from next door. Stending there enjoyin' being searched by this big gord. She hed walked pest the woman searcher end up till this tall chep with a big betton end insisted he ren his hends over her.

"Why thet hussy wis invited to a Royal Gordon Porty I

kint understend? I know why me end Hairy were invited. Its all may yerrs of secrifice fer cherity. All thim coffee porties for the poor sterving blecks in Efrica. Lest winter Ay put on heff a stone with all the vol-u-vonts end kinnepes Ay hed till devour for the | Etheopians alone.

"Enyway Ay was trying till avoid Veroniker and stepped intil this mud in me new shoes. By the time we got till the strawberry tent Ay was klebber till the knees. Then some ejit in a red helicopter nearly lended on top of us end sent may het flaying.

"Ay could hiv wept. End it wasn't even Princess Dienna who turned up. It was some Duke or somebody. Ay don't even know if he's related till the Royal Femily. Some wee slip of a lad brought may het beck. I was going till give a tip but somebody said he was a Minister for something et the N10. But Ay kin't keep treck of these Government cheps. Just when you stort till recognise one, he gets forgiven end whipped beck to Lunding.

"We ren intil Veroniker looking for the drinks tent. Ay told her therr wus no drinks tent. It was only strawberrys end cream. Like Wimbledon. She went off in a huff. Probably till get a flesk out of her gorter.

"You know. Ay think thet woman is an elcoholic. At home you niver see her without a gless in her hend. End who could forget thet Kerr-0-Bean cruise?

"Remember her end Edgar came with Hairy end me to Jamaker. She got herself invited till the Keptain's table and then drenk herself under it.

"Then when we got till Jamaker she turned up et the pool

60

porty et the hotel in one of thim string bikinis thet hed only a bit of cord for a beck. Ay tell you it was the biggest parcel thet string hed ever been tied round. Ay didn't know whur till look.

"Ay told her till her face thet she was a disgrace till Cherry velly. And she jist leffed. Leffed!! Like ther was something funny about Cherryvelly?

"Till tell you the truth Ay don't think she could hiv been from Cherryvelly originally. She was niver our kind of person. There was something of the gipsy about her. More like somebody from somewhur like Bengorr.

"Enyway the eposlutely worst thing she did in Jamaker was the night she pulled up her skirt end storted to limbo under this stick when there already wus a big heff neked bleck man limboing through from the other direction.

"Well!! Thenk God her poor husband Edgar was beck on the ship in a Becardi coma end wasn't there till witness thet spectacle when Veronicer end thet big bleck chep met in the middle. It was epsolutely indecent.

"If it hed been Cherryvelly instead of Jamaker somebody would hiv thrown a bucket of water over thim".

KERRIED HOME FROM THE WINE TASTING

by Billy Simpson

Hello Sendra, is thet you? Its me. Yer sister Egnes from Cherryvelly. Just ringing to scold you for not coming to may wee porty lest night. Ay niver believed for a minute you hed to stay home to wash the dog. Enyway you missed a great night. Toke about leff. Veroniker from next door was leffin' thet hord she nearly burst her Botox. Even may Hairy seemed to enjoy himself and you know how hord he is to amuse when visitors are drinking his Scotch.

Thet chep thet Veroniker brought with her was an epsolute hoot. He's retired from something but ay don't know whot exactly. Something ortistic ay fency because he talks like Brian Sewell, His name is Cyril and he got to know Veroniker when her kerried her home from a wine tasting evening at Cherryvelly Orts Club. You know Veroniker she spits nothing out.

Enyway, we hed a wee buffy laid on with semon petty and vol u vonts end things And nobody got sick on the meckeral dip this time, thenk God. Who would hev thought meckeral went off thet fest?

We played charades but Cyril was a bit obscure for us. Ay mean, who could be expected to get "The Four Horsemen of the

Apocalypse" from him gelloping around on his tip-toes traying to look like a skeleton. Hairy guessed it was "The Megic Roundabout".

Efter thet we played a game where everybody hed to name the faive famous people who hed given them the most pleasure. A bit like the 100 best Britons without the silly ones Neturally ay picked Dickie Velantine, Mett Monro and Deanna Durbin and people like thet. End of course Gary Grent. Mmmmmm. Remember him in "An Affurr till Remember" with Debra Kurr? Och Sendra, of course you do. We mitched off school to go to the matinee. We set through it twice and you were creying thet hord at the end, the meneger came round to see if you were all right. You sounded in such pain, he thought you'd fallen from the belcony.

Hairy's list was Jeck Nickless and a crowd of old film cowboys. John Wayne, Rendolph Scott end Joel McCrea. Not a woman on the list. So he took his list beck and added Eureka Johnson. Ay said "When did Eureka Johnson ever give you any pleasure? You've niver watched a programme she's been on."

He said just reading about her in the papers gave him pleasure. Ay think he'd bluffing. Ay mentioned her name lest week and he'd niver heard of her. If she wasn't flailing at a golf ball or shooting at Indians from a covered wegon, Hairy wouldn't know her from Edam.

Veroniker wrote out her list but nobody could read it. She'd hed the Gin shakes again and her scribble looked like a lie detector test. When it came to Cyril's list, we thought it would be people like Yen Goth or Pickesso. But strangely, no. He choose cheps like Graham Norton end Peter Mendleson. Hairy burst out leffing but ay shot him one of may glurrs. You hev to make allowances for ortistic people, ay believe. Though ay do think Veroniker is wasting her time on thet one.

VERONIKER USED HIM LIKE A RUDDER

by Billy Simpson

Stop leffing Sendra, it wasn't funny. Ay could be sued for a new yacht if thet man's memory ever comes beck. If it was enybody's fault it was Veroniker's. It was her wanted sailing lessons. Ay only went along for company. End everything was alright until we were about a mile off shore, then the wind dropped end we were bekemed This instructor chep was a right old sea-dog. His face wasn't exectly weather beaten. More like somebody hed beaten it with a barometer. Lucky Eddie McIntyre, he called himself, because, he said, he'd never lost a boat or a pessenger in 40 yerrs of sailing.

Ay esked how we'd get home if the wind didn't come beck and he said he had oars and Rolex for emergencies. Enyway Veroniker and I were sitting drinking some wayne to cool down. It was terrible hot. It was thet worm you could have frayed eggs on the deck. The sun was right in our faces so we thought if we pushed the boom to the other side of the boat the sail would give us some shade. So we did. Unfortunately we didn't know you are supposed to shout "Fore" or something and the boom hit Mr. McIntyre on the head and knocked him over the side.

We heard the splesh end him shouting some swear word from the water. Veroniker grebbed the tiller and tried to turn the boat around but the boom swung over again and hit Lucky Eddie on the head as he was climbing beck aboard.

Thurr was another big splesh and may new yachting outfit was epsolutely soaked. Neturally ay penicked. Ay didn't know if solt woter stained or not.

We looked over the side and saw Mr. McIntyre floating a few feet away. He was unconscious this time but didn't sink because he was wearing a life jecket. He was just bobbing about. Veroniker grebbed one of the oars and tried to ketch him but all she did was push him under a few times and I suspect may hev broken his nose.

I screamed at her to stop while I got a hold of Mr. McIntyre's old fishing line and kest it a few times to try to hook him. I finally meneged to get the hook through his ear lobe end began reeling him in. With nobody steering, the boat was just going around in circles so ay grebbed the tiller with one hend and hung onto the line with the other. Ay told Veroniker to go and get the flur gun and fire off a distress rocket. Well she fiddled for ages with thet thing before she got it loaded and then said "Whit do ay do now?" I screamed at her "Fire the demmed thing".

End she did. But she didn't point it et the sky. She fired it intil the deck of the boat. It bounced off; went over the side and lended on top of Mr. McIntyre's life jecket. Burning a hole and letting all the air out. Well. Sendra, as you ken imagine, by this time ay was ready to scream. So ay did.

Luckily the flames went out when Mr. McIntyre senk under the water. It took the two of us to pull him beck up. Ay still don't understand how thet ear of his stayed on. With all thet blood you'd hev thought it was henging by a thread. Enyway we got him beck to the surface at the sturn of the boat but he was too heavy for us to lift.

By this time Veroniker hed lost the hendle of the tiller so she leaned over the beck and tried to use Mr. McIntyre as a rudder to steer us beck to shore. Ay could see this was useless and got a hold of the flur gun again and hed another shot at a distress rocket. It was just bed luck thet the flur went through the main sail and set it on fire on the way pest. It is hord to credit thet we could miss the sky twice.

But thet flaming sail may hev saved us because the inshore lifeboat saw it and came out to rescue us. They took Mr. McIntyre to hospital. He was only cuncussed a bit. His nose was demeged and he'd swallowed a lot of sea woter. Heppily, he ken't remember a thing about the day's events. Mind you his left ear will be a bit longer than the other one, ay expect, but sailors sometimes wear an earring so maybe if he got a really big one.

Enyway, Sendra. ay ken't bring mayself to call him Lucky Eddie enymore. It might sound a bit sordonic in the circumstances.

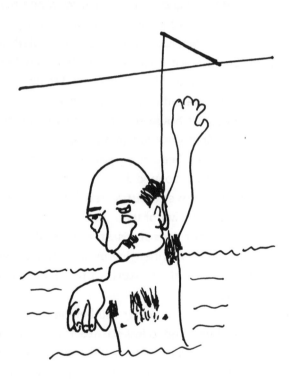

HONEYMOON IN VENUS

by Billy Simpson

Hello Sendra, Its me again, yer sister Egnes from Cherryvelly. Just ringing to tell you thet Hairy end I will be away for three weeks from next Setterday. Yeaass. Another wee trip abroad. We decided till go now instead of taking our usual Winter Holiday in Jenuary. Ay've gone off skiing. Efter thet eccident in Austria lest yerr ay don't think ay could face a nursery slope again. Remember when the beck of may jumper got caught on the cherr lift when I was getting off. End the lift just kept going. Ay was henging thurr dengling for heff an hour before they meneged to get me down.

Enyway Hairy never liked the snow end I ken't go with Veroniker because she was benned for life from the ski lodge efter thet .. er..incident on the slopes. You know, ay told you about it et the time. .... Yes I did. Oh. Didn't I?

Well it was a bit of a skendel but for once Veroniker was innocent. Yeaass. Hord till picture Veroniker being innocent of anything, I know.

Enyway we were stending around on this Elp waiting on the Embulencemen till clear the slopes of some chop who broke his enkle, end it was bitter cold. We were stomping our feet end flopping our orms till keep worm when the cold got till Veroniker's kidneys.

End them ski slopes hev very few facilities for women. Its easy for the men but not for women, particularly in them ski suits. Enyway, Veroniker said she was just bursting end couldn't wait eny longer. All thet beer I expect. She loped off behind some trees et the top of this wee hill. Ay told her till take her skis off before she took down her ski-suit, but would she listen? Well, she hed hordly hunkered down when her and the skis storted sliding down hill. She screamed et me till ketch her, but she was going too fest. She couldn't stend up and couldn't stop. She skiied beckwords right across the nursery slopes for about heff a mile. End the sight of her bare beckside caused epsolute chaos. But it wasn't her fault them other skiers kept kreshing intil trees. They should hev been looking where they were going.

Enyway lest week ay went intil town to book our holiday. There was this new young cutty behind the counter, looked like she should still be in school. Turns out she's the new essistant meneger.

Enyway when I told her I wanted to book two first kless tickets to Venus, she gave me this funny look. She seemed quite stortled in feet. "Venus"? she said. "Er.. hev you been there before?" "Yis", I said, "Hairy end I hed our honeymoon in Venus."

Well, she storted till look frightened. Ay glenced, behind me till see if a gengster with a gun hed come in till rob the place. Then I noticed her nodding to the security man on the door who came over end sort of hovered behind may beck. Very strange,

"What was Venus like?" she said in this nervous voice.

"Fentestic", ay said, "it was out of this world, Thet's why we are going beck again. Sort of a wee second honeymoon. We found the Venusians are very nice if you give them big tips. Especially those men with the big I'm poles end straw hets thet pole you around the kenels. Very romentic."

"Ah," she said, leffing like I'd said something funny. "Venice! In Italy! You want to go to Venice!" "Yes, thets what I said," I said. "Venus."

Thet's when ay realised the poor thing must hev ait hearing problem, bless her. Hairy always said thet loud disco music would tell on young people in later life. But you hev till give credit where its due. Thet wee girl hes done very well for herself for a hendicapped person.

IT TOOK THE ENEMEL OFF THE WOSHHEND BEESIN

by Billy Simpson

Hello Sendra, is thet you? It's me. Yer sister Egnes from Cherryvelly. Is may Torquin hidin' over with you and Semi? ....He's not. Well if he turns up you tell him to get beck home so ay kin kill him. Honestly Sendra, thet boy hes gone too forr this time. You know the number of times ay hev hed to hold may Hairy beck from strengling thet boy. He hes broken may hort more times then ay kurr to count, but.............. Whit's thet Sendra? ....Whit's he done now? Ay'll tell you whit he hes done. He hes almost kilt his father.

Yeaas. Poor Hairy is lying here at death's door waiting for the pairomedics to come and pump out his stomach. And all because of thet ejit Torquin's latest fentesy. He says he wants to be a mixologist. No Sendra. Ayd didn't know whit it was either. Epperently it is someone who mixes fency coketails.

Hairy leffed when he heard about it. Couldn't see Torquin getting a degree in any 'ology, even mixology. He's learning by e-mail or something. He sent away for some study disc to stick in his lep top. Says the mixing looks easy but juggling the bottles might take a bit of time.

Enyway, Veroniker from next door called in to borrow a cup of gin and when she heard about Torquin's latest scheme, she chellenged him to mix up a few fency coketails for us to tray.

Well, thet's all very fine for Veroniker, she's got a bionic stomach, but ay ken't touch elcohol while ay am on these teblets for thet... er... wee problem.. ay spoke to you about lest week.

.........No it still hesn't cleared up but it's not as itchy as it was. But to get beck to may Hairy. Torquin was delighted to mix some coketails from his lep top recipes. He raided our drinks kebinet and disappeared intil the kitchen for heff and hour. We could hear all this rettling and shaking and things being knocked over. He was always a clumbsy boy. Enyway he arrived out with this big tray of coketails. All different colours. Blue, pink, green, bleck - and one thet kept changing colour the more you watched it.

Neturally Veroniker got stuck in and they didn't seem to fizz on her. Even the one with the flames on top of it, Frenkly ay wondered about thet one because nobody put a metch to it. It sort of caught fire of its own volition.

Well you know what men are like. May Hairy tried to metch Veroniker drink for drink but ay could see the sweat breaking out on him efter he drenk thet bleck one. Next thing Torquin came rushing out of the kitchen looking eshen faced. Started craying and claiming it wasn't his fault. Something to do with the wrong message coming up on his lep top. Some of the coketails were OK to drink he said but some of them were for taking out stains. Right enough when Hairy opened his mouth to snarl his rage at Torquin, ay noticed thet his teeth were whiter than ay'd ever seen them. Then poor Hairy started foaming at the mouth and ren to the bethroom to be sick. Took all the enemel off the woshhend beesin.

Oh. Wait a minute Sendra. Ay hev to go. Ay hear the embulance now. Ay'd better go and make sure they pump Hairy first. If ay know Veroniker she'll be lying on her beck playing dead to trick some young pairomedic intil givng her the kiss of life.

DESESTER AT THE NATIVITY

by Billy Simpson

Hello Sendra, Is thet you? It's yer sister Egnes again from Cherry velly. Just ringing to worn you thet Rev Michael is efter you to play the piano at the Sunday School Nativity Play. I'm heving nothing to do with it this yerr. Not efter thet desester lest yerr when poor wee Simon, you know, the grendchild, our Victorr's youngest, was humiliated by thet maniac of a religious instructor.

What was his name? George Ebemethy or something like thet. Remember he taught the infants Scripture at Sunday School end played in thet jezz bend in his spare time. The sexephone. I didn't think jezz musicians could get intil a proper church. But enyway he was an epsolute tyrent with them wee children and he took a dislike till wee Simon for some reason. I know Simon kin be a wee rescel from time till time but ay thought Mr Ebemethy overreacted when Simon wanted till wear his cowboy het instead of thet turban thing. Ay mean, who knows whet Joseph wore on his head all them years ago?

But thet Ebemethy kept insisting on authenticity. You'd hev thought he was directing the peshion play at Oberammergau. I told him they were only children. Well! He turned and gave me such a glurr. If looks could kill I would hev been severely demeged.

He said Joseph hed till hev dignity and wee Simon hed better stop punching the Angel of the Lord or he'd be out on his erse. Fine language for a Sunday School Teacher thet. I called wee Simon over and told him thet he wasn't till hit the Angel of the Lord like thet no metter what she called him. Thet wee Melanie Crozier playing the Angel, called him a nose-picker. Well, Sendra, you know yourself thet all wee boys pick their noses. It's just thet he shouldn't hev been wiping his finger on her wings efterwords.

But Simon was no worse behaved then wee Rebecca McGuire who was playing Mary. Thet is one tough wee ticket. I don't know why they picked her for the Mother of the Lord. She'd hev been more convincing as King Herod, thet one. She kept stomping her foot and dregging wee Simon round by the ear. And God knows, Simon's ears are big enough already. He gets those from his mother's side of the family.

Thet's why the daughter-in-law Netelie always wears her hair round her face like a helmet. Till keep her ears down.

Enyway the rehearsal went on all eftemoon end Simon end Rebecca were fighting the bit out all the way. I could see Mr Ebemethy was coming till the end of his tether. Ay think thet man suffers with his nerves, you know.

When it came till the scene where Mary cradles baby Jesus, thet wicket wee girl said, "I don't want a boy. I want a wee baby girl and I'm calling her Kylie."

Thet's when Simon grebs her by the neck and say, "It's a boy and I'm calling him Jason.

Well, Mr Ebemethy went beserk and kept screaming the Lord's name at them. Heff time I didn't know whether he was prompting them or blespheming. At this point the Angel of the Lord took off one of her wings and storted hitting poor Simon over the head with it. Thet was when he tore off her other wing and knocked her off the stage. Well kin you blame the child?

I mean Simon's only five years old. But you would hev expected better from Rebecca and Melaine. I mean they are five-end-a-heff if they're a day.

ALL PORT OF LIFE'S" RICH PETTERN

by Billy Simpson

"Hello Sendra, is thet you? Its your sister Egnes from Cherry velly... Hello... Hello. Ur youse therr? I kint hear you... Heng on a minute. Ay'll tell Tarquin to turn down a his hay-fi. Tarquin, Mummy's on the phone so would youse mind torning thet recket down. There thets better. Enyway Sendra ay wonder if you would maynd hiving mother for Christmas. Ay know, ay know, its may turn but she's draving us all med.

"Ay think Cheeryvelly is too hay-tech for mother. She'd be much heppier with you in Bellybean. Ay think she's pining for the sight of a jawbox again. May dishwasher is beyond her. Ay keep telling her everything in may house is autometic, but she keeps opening the front and pouring basins of water intil it. End she's been up with the garage door twice.

"But lest Seterday was the worrrst. She decided to hiv a beth so ay got her intil our Jerkuzi. Oh yes. Don't you hiv thim in Bellybean? You must come over for a dip sometime. No it doesn't hiv a diving board? Ur you being sercestic Sendra? Enywey the Jerkuzi was an epsolute disester. When the water started to bubble up round her she thought her old trouble hed come beck.

"She lept out of thurr like a scalded ket and ran out through our new conserve-a-tory intil the gordon. Epsolutely NECKET. Ay hid to tell the neighbours she was a stippergrem lukin for the rugby club.

73

"End you know mother. You kint talk till 'er. She snepped the nose off me this morning when Ay told her Hairy and Ay are flaying to over to Lunding for Herrods sale. She sid Ay was all fur coat and no knickers.

"Efter all Ay've done fer thet woman! Enyway, the whole thing came till a head over the setelite television. Y'know we've got rid of thet big dish from the gordon. Hairy said it med the place look like a radorr station. We've got one of the little bleck one's now. Very discreet. You could hordly see it on our big roof.

"Alright. Don't snep at me Sendra, aim coming till thet. We were all sitting down watching Skay, it was a progromme with Robin Day in it. You know. The crebbit one with the glesses. Well suddenly mother says 'Isn't he a bit old till be up in one of them things?' 'Whit things?' aye said. Thim setelite things' she siz.

"Well I had till leff. 'Mother dear,' ay siz, 'Did youse think thet Robin Day was flaying round in space on the Storship Enterprise with Keptain Kirk?'

"So Ay explained it was only a wee ball in the sky and thet Robin Day was bounching his photo off it from Lunding. "Who's up thurr driving it?," she siz. "Nobody's driving it," Ay siz. "It's autometic, like the dishwasher."

"WELL! She lets out this scream you could hiv heard in Bengorr. Then she got under the coffee table and sid thet if nobody wiz driving the setelite it could fall on our house. Honestly! She's med as a hetter.

"Enyway Hairy and Ay talked it over and we think she would be heppier with youse for Christmas. I mean your house his bin very low-tech since they repossessed your guess cooker. (CLICK.)

... Hello. Sendra. Sendra... If youse hiv cut me off you'll niver see the inside of may split-level again, sister or no sister".

TORQUIN AND THE RAIN FORESTS

by Billy Simpson

Hello Sendra,
Is thet you? Listen, you will hev to come over here to 'Wuthering
Cherries' and try and tolk some sense intil Torquin. Hairy and I
kin't do a thing with him. He has got
involved with this Hippy girl
and she hes turned his
head...... I know, I
know... it wasn't
much of a
head till
begin with,
but he's
drayving
us med.

She hes
got him intil
one of these
clubs thet think
the Earth is their
Mother, end I'm being
driven till distraction trying
to get him till eat. He says he won't eat
anything thet hes a brain or a central nervous system.
      I've spent all eftemoon scouring the shelves at Morks
trying till find something stupid enough for him till eat.
      When we got home we found all our pettio furniture
piled up in the middle of the gordon. Torquin said it was a sin till

75

use wood for anything while the rain forest is disappearing off the mep. I thought he meant Belvoir Pork, but apparently it's in South America. Y'know. Where Carmen Merenda came form. Hairy went med and grebbed poor Torquin by the throat, but I got Hairy away.

"Torquin dear," I says, "our gordon furniture came from trees thet were dying enyway. They were growing in Glengormley and hed lost the will till live. You know yourself Sendra, there is a dreft comes round thet mountain would clean corn.

Enyway, I got them both calmed down but now I've got this Hippy girl coming over for tea end I don't know what till give them. She won't even eat Brussel sprouts in case it robs kebbage of its young, Hairy says just give them a beg of gress each and leave them till it, I but I've been in a penic all day.

The lest time she called for him to go to some Dendylion Support Group meeting she told me off for wearing perfume end lipstick. " Said I was committing Nasal Fecism end demeging the ozone layer. Then she took the huffs when I said, "How do you feel about soap?"

Well it was her haircut put me off. She hes prectically shaved her head. Just like the fet one in the Three Stooges. I thought it was to get rid of nits but Torquin says it's the Sinead O'Connor look.

At the same time she is not a bed looking wee girl, just very intense. Efter all she is from Strenmillis, so you hev till make allowances.

End as well as everything else, Torquin hes been bedgering

me to kerry a Donor Cord. Said I could save lives if I ever got run over. Imagine saying a thing like thet till your mother.

Enyway, they don't have Gold Donor Cords, because I esked. So your bits and pieces could be going till anybody. I wouldn't like somebody walking around with bits of me in them and taking them till places I wouldn't be seen dead in.

Which reminds me, Veroniker end I were in town today for the first time in yonks. End you wouldn't believe what they've done till Enderson and McAuley's. Big pictures of Donald Duck on the windows edvertising this new Disney shop. Ay couldn't be more tremetised if they turned Herod's intil a bingo perlour. I didn't want till go near it, because I still get very emotional about it, you know, but Veroniker insisted we went intil this place called Hebitett on the comer.

Veroniker thought it was wonderful and bought rings round her, but it looked like an Ereb Market till me. It was all a bit Chennel Four, it you know what I mean. It'll take a bit of getting used till.

Enyway Sendra, I want you to nip over and hev a wee talk with Torquin. Explain to him he has till eat something. Tell him a Veda loaf doesn't hev a nervous system but I do.

KENT STOP MOTHER TAKING THE TEBLETS

by Billy Simpson

Hello Sendra,

Is thet you? Its me, yer sister Egnes from Cherryvelly. Ay am ringing to worn you about the latest feasco concerning mother. The matron at the home was on till me again about her. Honestly, thet woman will be the death of me. Ay ken't take much more of this. Ay am crecking up. Efter everything ay hev done for thet woman, she still seems determined to break may hort.

..........Whit's thet Sendra? .... Whit's she been up to now? .... Ay'll tell you whit she hes been up to. Our mother hes been forging Euro notes.. Yeaaaas. Forging Euros. ......End you kin stop thet giggling Sendra. This is no leffing metter. Ay didn't think mother even knew whit a Euro was, but according to matron, he mind is as shorp as a teck at the moment. Some new experimental teblets she's on.

Efter all thim yerrs when she hordly knew her own femily and kept thinking you, me and your Auntie Morgoret were the Endrews Sisters come to entertain her. NOW she gets her mind beck.

When ay first heard she hed improved, ay said to mayself, "Thenk God. We won't hev till sing 'Boogie Woogie Bugle Boy of Company B' any more to humour the old bet.

Heving to sing it was bed enough but if your Auntie Morgoret hed to do thet jitterbugging one more time ay don't think her hort could stend it.

Now her mind is working again it just means she's smort as well as med. Ay blame thim teblets the doctor put her on. Remember he esked our permission to try them out in her to see if they helped her memory. Ay don't know why they picked mother to test them on. Ay expect there's some law against using rets.

Enyway, the other day Matron caught mother and some of the other old folk in the home, playing poker. Yeaas. Poker!! But when she looked closer she noticed thet while the other residents where putting real faive and 10p coins in the kitty, mother was using bits of printed paper. Sendra, you will niver believe whit thet old witch did! She cut coupons out of newspapers. You know the kind. '50pc off sale prices' and 'ten pc off a bor of soap'. Then she hed some accomplice run off copies on a photocopier. .... Yeaaas! The old devil. Enyway she conned the other old fools into thinking these were veluable Euros. She got away with it because none of thim hed seen a real Euro. Mind you one old doll did esk, why one side of the Euros was blenk. Mother told him thet it was blenk because Britain hed'nt joined yet. When we join, she said, they'll print ours on the other side.

Now to be furr to mother, she was offering a better exchange rate than the benks. Or it would hev been if they hedn't only been bits of paper.

Well Hairy and ay were summoned to the home and believe me, Sendra, ay gave mother a good talking to. I made her give all the old dears beck their pension money. And Mr. Moffett his long Johns and Mrs. O'Hera, her corsets. (Although ay don't think they were playing for money, the night they lost thurr undergarments. Frenkly, Sendra. ay shuddered to esk.)

Mother was always a henful but she's getting worse. When we spoke till the doctor who was testing the teblets on her, he said he was astonished. They shouldn't hev hed such a morked effect. He suspects thet mother may have just been pretending not to know us before, because she bet some of the other residents she could get you, me and Aunt Morgoret till sing like the Endrews Sisters.

You know, ay heff believe him. Because when ay came

79

beck to her room, thurr was may Hairy slepping his thigh and singing "Bless Yore Beautiful Hide" from "Seven Brides for Seven Brothers". She'd told him he was the picture of Howard Keel, and he was thet flettered he fell for it.

When she saw me stending at the door, an evil glint came in her eye, and she cried "Oh. Its Kethryn Grayson. Now you and Howard can sing something from 'Showboat.'

Honestly ay will swing for thet woman yet........Whit's thet Sendra..... Well...er..yes. Just a few verses of 'Make Believe'. Well you know ay was born for thet port but when Cherryvelly Opera Group put it on they always kest me as Big Memmy.